FROM GENERATION TO GENERATION

REFLECTIONS

A Jewish Grandparent's Gift of Memories

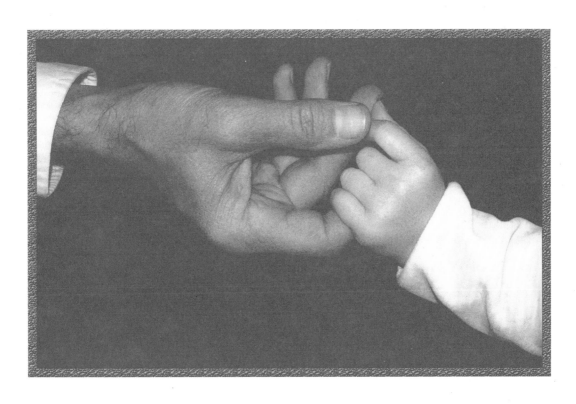

Ronald H. Isaacs and Leora W. Isaacs

KTAV PUBLISHING HOUSE, INC.
in association with
HAZAK
The UNITED SYNAGOGUE OF CONSERVATIVE JUDAISM'S
Organization For Mature Jews

The authors gratefully acknowledge permission to reprint the following:

Sam Levenson, "Sam Levenson's Ethical Will and Testament to His Grandchildren and Children Everywhere," reprinted from ETHICAL WILLS: A MODERN JEWISH TREASURY, copyright © 1983 by Schocken Books.
Originally appeared in WOMAN'S DAY, May 3, 1977. Copyright © 1976 by Sam Levenson. Reprinted by permission of Literistic, Ltd.

Library of Congress Cataloging-in-Publication Data

Isaacs, Ronald H.
  Reflections : a Jewish grandparents' gift of memories / Ronald H. Isaacs, Leora W. Isaacs. -- Rev. ed.
     p. cm.
ISBN 978-0-88125-965-0
1. Genealogy--Forms. 2. Jews--Genealogy. I. Isaacs, Leora W. II. Title. III. Isaacs, Ronald H.
CS24.I83 2007
929'.1072089924--dc22

2007027644

Published by
KTAV Publishing House, Inc.
930 Newark Avenue
Jersey City, NJ 07306
Email: bernie@ktav.com
www.ktav.com
(201) 963-9524
Fax (201) 963-0102

Printed in China

In memory of our fathers,
David Isaacs and Joshua Weinstein,
who planted seeds of goodness
and wisdom for their grandchildren

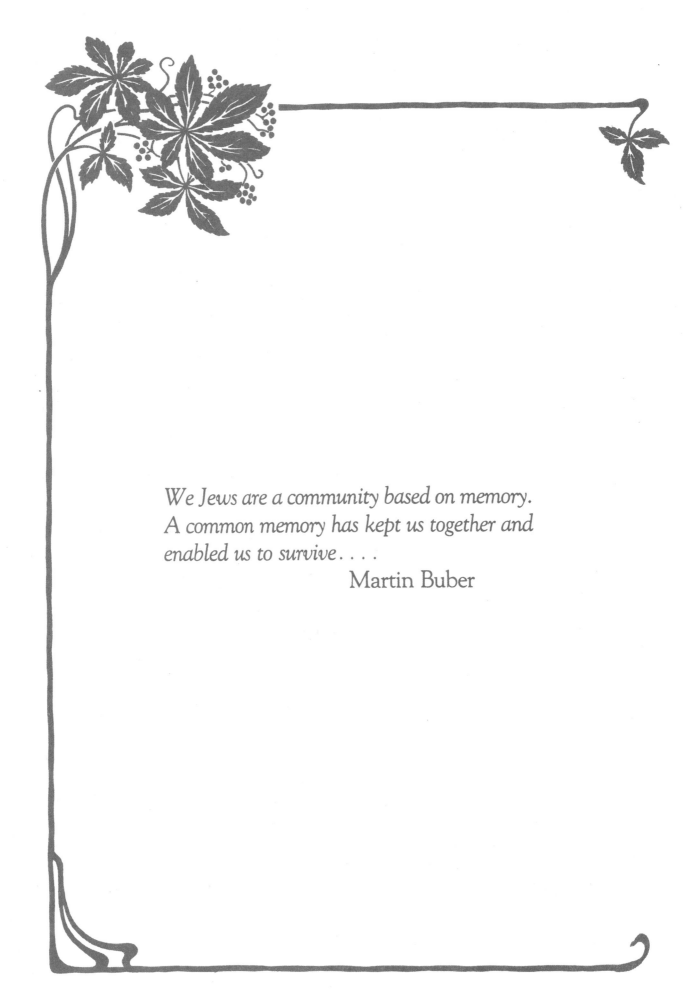

We Jews are a community based on memory.
A common memory has kept us together and
enabled us to survive. . . .
Martin Buber

MAY GOD BLESS YOU FROM ZION;
MAY YOU SHARE THE PROSPERITY OF
JERUSALEM ALL THE DAYS OF YOUR LIFE,
AND LIVE TO SEE YOUR CHILDREN'S
CHILDREN. MAY ALL BE WELL WITH ISRAEL.

Psalm 128:6

וּרְאֵה בָנִים לְבָנֶיךָ שָׁלוֹם עַל יִשְׂרָאֵל

CONTENTS

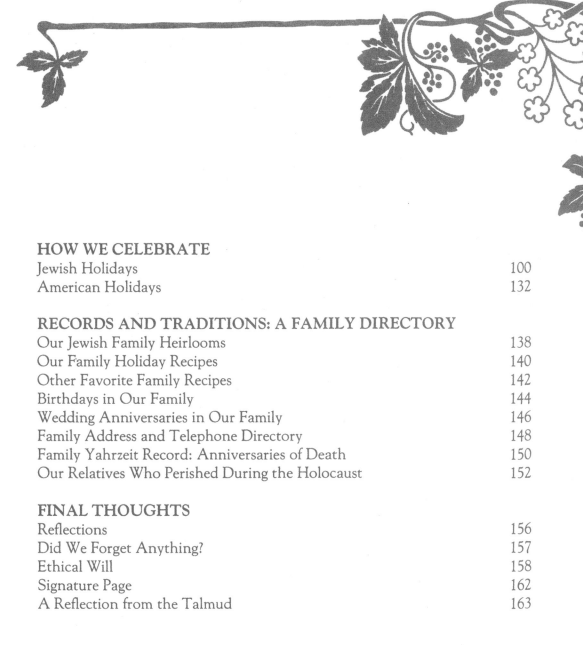

PREFACE

You and your grandchildren share a very special relationship. It is based on unconditional love and is nurtured by common heritage and experiences. Because of this, each of you holds precious what the other values.

This book reflects that reciprocal relationship. By making entries in it, you can record and transmit your family history, culture, values, thoughts, feelings, and aspirations to your grandchild. You also have opportunities to collect mementos and to respond to the important events in your grandchild's life.

No doubt you and your grandchildren love to talk about your
experiences and each other. We
hope this book will become a
vehicle for intergenerational communication between you. If you
work on it when you are together, while you are making entries in the book, your grandchild
may respond with illustrations,
comments, comparisons, and con-
trasts, making the compilation of
this heirloom an interactive proj-
ect. Of course, you may also
complete the book on your own
and present it to your grandchildren.

In a sense, the goal of this book is
to root your grandchildren in
your family heritage and to ex-
press how they are the flowering
of your family tree. For you, as
grandparents, it offers the opportunity to look back and forward,
to bridge past and future generations. The questions and state-
ments in this book will provide a
framework for you to tell your
grandchildren the story of your
family.

R. H. I.
L. W. I.

Dear Grandparents,

As you flip through the pages of this book, you will notice that they contain several kinds of questions and places to record many types of information about your family. There are places to record your family tree, your family hsitory, your reminiscences about milestones in the lives of your children, and your memories of holiday observances and celebrations. The questions on each page of the book are only intended to guide your reminiscence. Please feel free to use them as an outline, adding to them or skipping those that do not pertain to you.

At the end of each section there is a place for a signature. Grandmother may wish to complete some sections, while Grandfather may complete others. The signature will let future readers of this heirloom know who completed a particular section.

Some sections, especially those about family history, may require a little research. Completing this book may provide the perfect opportunity to interview family members and to find out more about your roots. There are a number of places in which you are asked to recall an event by its Hebrew date. If you need help in determining these dates, we suggest that you consult the 2,000-year calendar in the *Encyclopedia Judaica* or ask your local rabbi for assistance.

We know that you will probably not wish to mount irreplaceable family documents and photographs in this book. We therefore suggest that you mount copies of such photographs and documents (*ketubahs*) and keep the originals in a secure place.

You will also note that there is a pocket in the back of the book in which you can place a disk of your video or photographic memories.

Reflections: A Jewish Grandparents' Gift of Memories is not meant to be completed all at once. You may wish to complete the portions related to when your grandchild is born when you receive the book, then go back to fill in the parts about holiday celebrations and milestones in your grandchild's life as your grandchild grows. As your grandchild matures, you might share your reflections with him or her and ask your grandchild to write or draw his or her reactions in the specified places in the book. Of course, it is possible to complete the book in a shorter period of time as well.

This book is intended as a personalized heirloom that grandparents may present to a grandchild when it is completed. You will note that many of the sections, such as those about family history and holidays, may apply to several grandchildren in the family, but other sections pertain to only one grandchild. You may want to keep copies of the information necessary for the general sections, should you wish to present a book of reflections to each grandchild.

We hope that your experiences in completing this book will be enjoyable and rewarding ones both for you and your family.

R. H. I.
L. W. I.

TRACING OUR ROOTS

Our Family Tree
Your Great-Great-Grandparents (My Grandparents)
Your Great-Grandparents (My Parents)

Dear _____,

Like all families, you have a rich heritage, half from your mom's side and half from your dad's. Together you have inherited so much! This book will document one side of the family. I hope you will learn about the other side of the family as well.

Our Family Tree

OUR GRANDPARENTS

_____

| Your great-great grandmother | Your great-great grandfather | Your great-great grandmother | Your great-great grandfather |

OUR PARENTS

_____
Your great-grandmother

Your great-grandfather

Us

_____
Your grandmother

Our children
(including your
parents)   _____   _____

Our grandchildren
(including you)

_____   _____

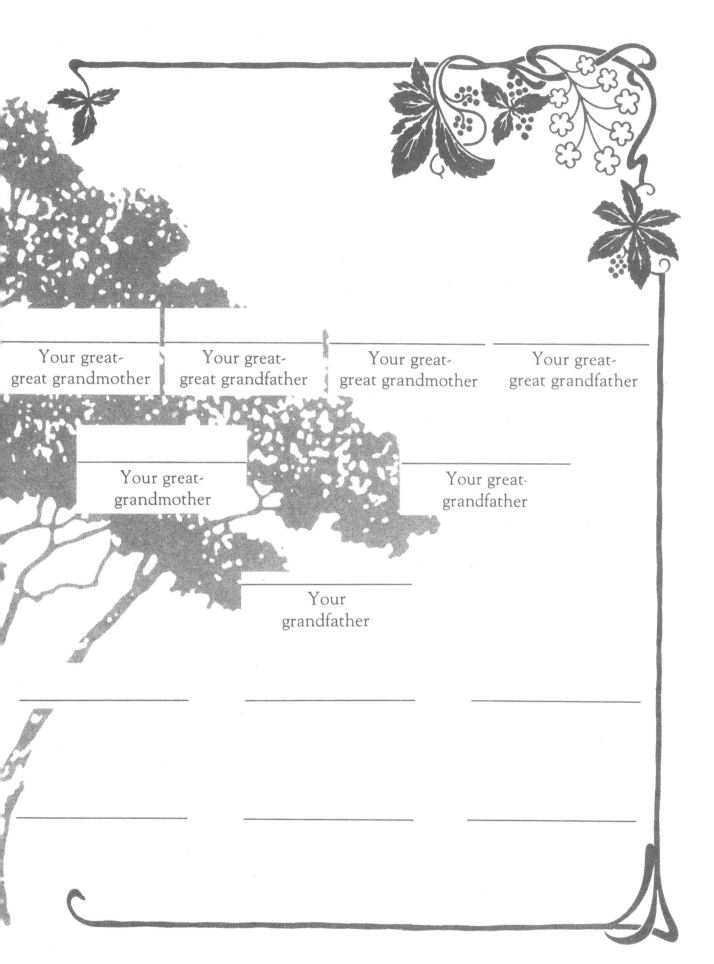

Your great-
great grandmother

Your great-
great grandfather

Your great-
great grandmother

Your great-
great grandfather

Your great-
grandmother

Your great-
grandfather

Your
grandfather

It is fun to trace family appearances through the generations. Here is a photographic album of our family tree.

Our grandparents
(Your great-great grandparents)

Our parents
(Your great-grandparents)

Us
(Your grandparents)

Our children
(Your parents, aunts, and uncles)

Our grandchildren
(You, your brothers and sisters, and your cousins)

Note to grandparents: Photography was not common until the late 1800s, so it may be difficult to find pictures of your grandparents. It is recommended that you include *copies* of your family photos rather than the originals.

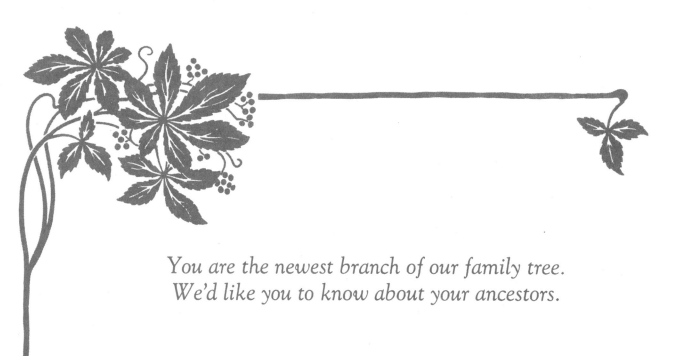

You are the newest branch of our family tree.
We'd like you to know about your ancestors.

YOUR GREAT-GREAT-GRANDPARENTS
(My Grandparents)

My grandparents planted for me.
Now I plant for my grandchildren. (Ta'anit 23a)

On your grandmother's side of the family:

My mother's father was named _____ (_____ in Hebrew),

and we called him _____.   My mother's mother was named

_____ (_____ in Hebrew). The name we called her

was _____. They came from _____ and lived

_____. My grandfather earned his living

as a _____and my grandmother

was a _____. They had _____

children named _____

_____.

I remember that my grandfather _____
_____
_____.

I remember that my grandmother _____
_____
_____.

The things I best liked doing with my grandparents were _____
_____
_____.

Sometimes, people resemble their ancestors. In our family, I am reminded of my grandfather and grandmother by the way _____
_____.

In our family, the people named after my grandfather and grand-mother are _____
_____.

Some other things I'd like you to know about my mother's parents are _____
_____.

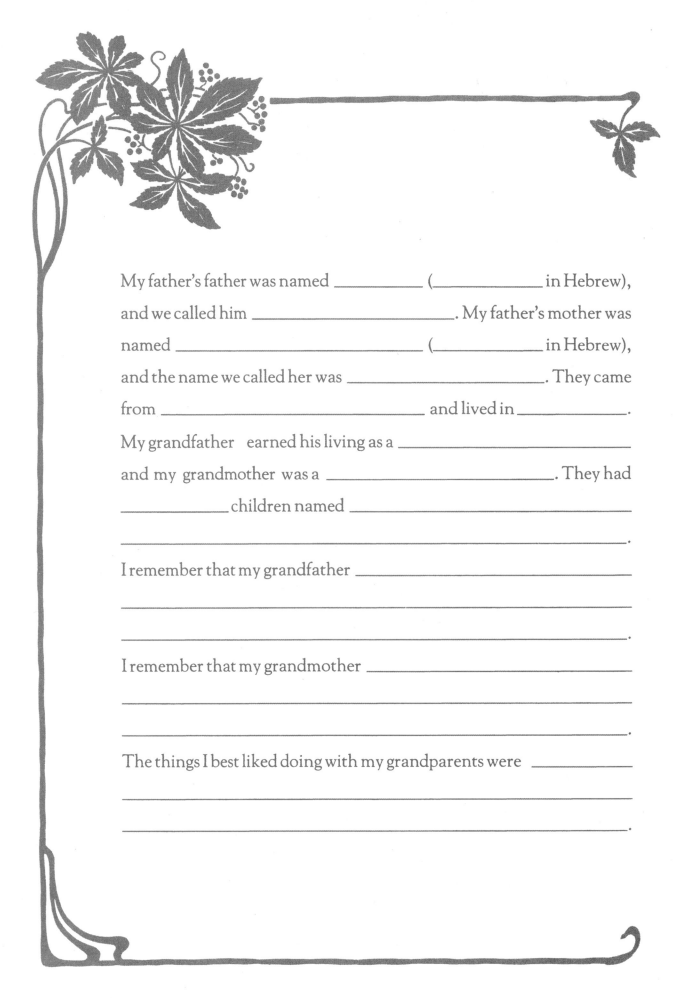

My father's father was named _____ (_____ in Hebrew),
and we called him _____. My father's mother was
named _____ (_____ in Hebrew),
and the name we called her was _____. They came
from _____ and lived in _____.
My grandfather   earned his living as a _____
and my grandmother was a _____. They had
_____children named _____
_____.

I remember that my grandfather _____
_____
_____.

I remember that my grandmother _____
_____
_____.

The things I best liked doing with my grandparents were _____
_____
_____.

Sometimes, people resemble their ancestors. In our family, I am reminded of my grandfather and grandmother by the way _____
_____.

In our family, the people named after my grandfather and grandmother are _____
_____
_____.

Some other things I'd like you to know about my father's parents
are _____
_____
_____.

_____

(Signed)

11

Your Great-Great-Grandparents
(My Grandparents)

On your grandfather's side of the family:

My mother's father was named _____ (_____ in Hebrew),
and we called him _____.   My mother's mother was named
_____ (_____ in Hebrew). The name we called her
was _____. They came from _____ and lived
in _____. My grandfather earned his living
as a _____ and my grandmother was
a _____. They had _____ children
named _____
_____.

I remember that my grandfather _____
_____
_____.

I remember that my grandmother _____
_____
_____.

The things I best liked doing with my grandparents were _____
_____
_____.

Sometimes, people resemble their ancestors. In our family, I am reminded of my grandfather and grandmother by the way _____
_____.

In our family, the people named after my grandmother and grandfather are _____
_____
_____.

Some other things I'd like you to know about my mother's parents
are _____
_____
_____.

My father's father was named _____ (_____ in Hebrew),
and we called him _____. My paternal grandmother
(father's mother) was named _____ (_____ in Hebrew).
The name we called her was _____. They came
from _____ and lived in _____.

My grandfather earned his living as a _____

and my grandmother was a _____. They had

_____ children named _____

_____.

I remember that my grandfather _____

_____

_____.

I remember that my grandmother _____

_____

_____.

The things I best liked doing with my grandparents were _____

_____

_____.

Sometimes, people resemble their ancestors. In our family, I am reminded of my grandfather and grandmother by the way _____

_____.

In our family, the people named after my grandmother and grand-father are _____

_____

_____.

Some other things I'd like you to know about my father's parents are _____

_____

_____.

_____

_____

_____

_____

(Signed)

PICTURES OF
GRANDMOTHER'S GRANDPARENTS

My mother's mother   My mother's father

My father's mother

My father's father

Note to grandparents: You may mount photographs of your grandparents on this page and/or you may ask your grandchild to draw portraits or illustrations based on your descriptions.

PICTURES OF
GRANDFATHER'S GRANDPARENTS

My mother's mother

My mother's father

My father's mother   My father's father

Note to grandparents: You may mount photographs of your grandparents on this page and/or you may ask your grandchild to draw portraits or illustrations based on your descriptions.

YOUR GREAT-GRANDPARENTS
(My Parents)

On your grandmother's side of the family:

My mother was born in _____ in the

year_____. She was named _____

(_____ in Hebrew). She used to tell me stories

about when she was growing up. I especially remember the story she told

about _____

_____

_____

_____.

Your parent called her _____.

My father was born in _____ in the

year _____. He was named _____

(_____ in Hebrew). I remember the stories my

father told me about when he was growing up, especially about _____

_____

_____

_____

_____ .

Your parent called him _____ .

The way my parents met was _____

_____

_____

_____ .

_____ . They were

married in _____ in the year
  place

_____ , and settled in _____ .

My father earned his living as a _____ and my

mother was a _____ . They had _____ children

named _____

_____

_____ .

I remember my father's special talents and hobbies were _____

_____ and my mother's were _____

_____.

As a family, we used to love to _____

_____

_____

_____.

Some of the most important things that I learned from my parents

were _____

_____

_____

_____.

Nowadays in our family, I am reminded of my mother and my father by

the way _____

_____

_____

_____.

The people in our family who were named after my mother and father

are _____

_____ .

Some other things I'd like you to know about my parents are _____

_____

_____

_____

_____

_____

_____

_____

_____

_____ .

_____

(Signed)

YOUR GREAT-GRANDPARENTS
(My Parents)

On your grandfather's side of the family:

My mother was born in _____ in the
year _____. She was named _____
(_____ in Hebrew). She used to tell me stories
about when she was growing up. I especially remember the story she told
about _____
_____
_____
_____
_____.

Your parent called her _____.

My father was born in _____ in the

year_____. He was named _____

(_____ in Hebrew). I remember the stories my father

told me about when he was growing up, especially _____

_____

_____

_____. Your parent called him_____.

The way my parents met was _____

_____

_____

_____

_____. They were mar-

ried in _____ in the year _____,
place
and settled in _____.My father earned his living as a

_____ and my mother was a _____.

They had _____ children named _____

_____.

I remember my father's special talents and hobbies were_____

_____ and my mother's were_____

_____.

As a family, we used to love to _____

_____

_____.

Some of the most important things that I learned from my parents were

_____

_____

_____.

Nowadays in our family, I am reminded of my mother and my father by

the way_____

_____

_____

_____.

The people in our family who were named after my mother and father are

_____

_____.

Some other things I'd like to tell about my parents are _____

_____

_____

_____

_____

_____

_____

_____

_____.

_____

(Signed)

PICTURES OF
GRANDMOTHER'S PARENTS

Mother

Father

Write your own caption: _____

_____

Write your own caption: _____

_____

PICTURES OF
GRANDFATHER'S PARENTS

Mother   Father

Write your own caption: _____   Write your own caption: _____

_____   _____

Note to grandparents: You may mount copies of photographs on this page and/or you may
ask your grandchild to draw portraits or illustrations based on your descriptions.

ALL ABOUT YOUR GRANDPARENTS

Grandparents' Childhood
Jewish Education and Religious Milestones
Grandmother as a Young Woman
Grandfather as a Young Man
Our Wedding and Marriage: Grandmother and Grandfather Together
Grandmother Looking Back
Grandfather Looking Back

GRANDPARENTS' CHILDHOOD

We'd like to share with you some of our memories of when we were growing up. We thought it might be fun to compare some facts about our childhood with facts about yours and your parents to see the similarities and differences.

Grandmother

Name, Hebrew Name, Nickname _____

Date of Birth (English & Hebrew) _____

Height and weight at birth _____

Eye color _____

Hair color (as child) _____

Place of birth _____

Brothers and sisters
(in order of birth)
_____

_____

Some special memories about
our brothers and sisters
_____

_____

_____

_____

Grandfather	My child (Your parent)	My grandchild (You)

GRANDPARENTS' CHILDHOOD

Grandmother

SCHOOL DAYS

Name(s) of school(s) _____

Memories of school(s) _____

_____

_____

Favorite subject(s) _____

Least favorite subject(s) _____

Favorite teacher(s) _____

Best friend(s) _____

What we enjoyed doing together _____

_____

_____

School activities (clubs) _____

_____

FAVORITES & PREFERENCES

Favorite sports _____

Awards _____

_____

_____

Favorite songs _____

Favorite toys _____

Grandfather	My child (Your parent)	My grandchild (You)

GRANDPARENTS' CHILDHOOD

Grandmother

Favorite games/activities _____

_____

_____

Favorite amusements (movies, radio _____
or television shows, etc.)

_____

_____

Favorite actors, singers, teams, _____
cartoon characters, etc.

_____

_____

Pets _____

Favorite foods _____

Most disliked foods _____

Most memorable news events
during my lifetime

_____

_____

_____

The longest trip I took (transportation,
destination, what I did there) _____

_____

_____

_____

Neighbors _____

Grandfather	My child (Your parent)	My grandchild (You)

GRANDPARENT'S CHILDHOOD

Grandmother

IMPORTANT PEOPLE, PLACES & EVENTS (CONT.)

Family friends (including adults) _____

_____

_____

Favorite relatives (aunts, uncles, cousins, etc.) and what we especially liked about them

_____

_____

Most memorable summer vacations (including summer camp)

_____

_____

HABITS & FOLKLORE

Habits (e.g., thumb sucking, falling asleep in car, hair twirling, etc.)

_____

_____

Family superstitions _____

_____

HOBBIES TALENTS

Hobbies _____

Talents _____

_____

Languages (spoken and read)_____

Grandfather	My child (Your parent)	My grandchild (You)

PICTURES OF
GRANDPARENTS AS CHILDREN

Grandmother

Write your own caption: _____

_____

Grandfather

Write your own caption: _____

_____

Note to grandparents: You may mount copies of photographs on this page and/or you may ask your grandchild to draw portraits or illustrations based on your descriptions.

The Torah is a Tree of Life to those who take hold of it,
and those who support it will be enriched. (Proverbs 3:18)

עֵץ חַיִּים הִיא לַמַּחֲזִיקִים בָּהּ וְתֹמְכֶיהָ מְאֻשָּׁר

Jewish Education
and Religious Milestones

Grandmother

I was named after _____. I received my

Jewish education at _____

_____.

The things I remember most about my Jewish education were _____

_____.

My favorite Bible story was _____

and my favorite Bible character was _____ because

_____

_____.

My favorite Jewish holiday was _____ because

_____

_____.

My favorite Jewish book was _____.

The name of our synagogue was _____.

When I think about our synagogue, I remember _____

_____

_____.

Our rabbi was named _____. What I

remember most about him is _____

_____

_____.

I celebrated becoming an adult Jewish woman by _____

_____

_____.

I continued my Jewish education by _____

_____

_____.

Other memories of my Jewish education and milestones in my life as a

Jew include _____

_____

_____

_____.

_____

(Signed)

43

Jewish education is more important than anything. (Mishnah Peah I:1)

תַּלְמוּד תּוֹרָה כְּנֶגֶד כּוּלָם

Jewish Education
and Religious Milestones

Grandfather

My Hebrew name _____ was given to me at
my Brit Milah (Bris) on _____.

Hebrew date.

My godparents (Sandek and Kvater) were _____.

I was named after _____. I received my

Jewish education at_____.

My most memorable religious school teacher was _____

because _____

_____

The thing I most remember about my Jewish education was _____

_____

_____

My favorite Bible story was _____ and my

favorite Biblical character was _____ because

_____

_____

My favorite Jewish holiday was _____ because

_____

My favorite Jewish book was _____.

The name of our synagogue was _____.

When I think about our synagogue, I remember _____

_____

_____.

Our rabbi was named _____. What I

remember most about him is _____

_____

_____.

On my Bar Mitzvah my Torah portion was _____ and my

Haftorah was _____.

In my Bar Mitzvah speech, I talked about _____

_____

_____.

We celebrated my becoming a Bar Mitzvah by _____

_____

_____.

The things I remember most about my Bar Mitzvah were _____

_____

_____

_____.

I continued my Jewish education after my Bar Mitzvah by _____

_____

_____.

Other memories of my Jewish education and Bar Mitzvah include

_____

_____.

_____
(Signed)

PICTURE OF GRANDMOTHER
AS A STUDENT, AGE 12–13.

Write your own caption: _____

_____

Note to grandparents: You may mount a copy of a photograph on this page and/or you may ask your grandchild to draw a portrait or illustration based on your description.

PICTURE OF GRANDFATHER
AS A STUDENT, AGE 12–13.

Write your own caption: _____

_____

Note to grandparents: You may mount a copy of a photograph on this page and/or you may ask your grandchild to draw a portrait or illustration based on your description.

GRANDMOTHER
AS A YOUNG WOMAN

I began high school in the year _____. I attended _____

_____ school in _____,
city/state/country

_____

My favorite subjects were _____,

and my least favorite subjects were _____.

I celebrated my Confirmation at _____,
city/state/country

_____ in the year _____.

I especially remember my teacher _____,

because _____

_____

_____

_____

The names of my best friends were _____,

_____

We enjoyed doing many things together including _____

_____

_____

I'll never forget the time _____

_____

_____

_____

I was especially proud of _____

_____ .

I participated in activities, sports, and clubs such as _____

_____

_____ .

The names of our teams/clubs were _____

_____ .

My position was _____ .

Some of our best programs/activities/games were _____

_____

_____ .

The elections/awards I won were for _____

_____ .

In those days, my favorite song was _____ ,

my favorite dance was _____ , and my favorite

entertainment (show, program, movie, game, etc.) was _____ .

My favorite book as a teenager was _____ .

I was a fan of _____ .

The most popular fads were _____

_____ .

The important world news events of the time were _____

_____

_____.

I remember _____

_____

_____

_____.

I finished high school in _____ and went on to
                                   date
_____. My first "real job" was _____.

My salary was $ _____ per _____. The first election

I voted in was in the year _____, and the candidate I voted

for was _____. _____

was elected. The way I came to choose my occupation of _____

_____ was _____

_____

_____.

I got my training _____

_____

_____.

As a young woman I belonged to _____

_____

(clubs and organizations). The Jewish organizations I belonged to were

_____

_____.

Some of my activities included _____

_____

_____.

I met your grandfather in _____. I'll never

date

forget how we met! _____

_____

_____

_____.

The things that attracted me to him were _____

_____

_____.

When we dated _____

_____

_____.

The things I remember most about our courtship were _____

_____

_____

_____

_____.

Other memories of my young adulthood include _____

_____

_____

_____

_____.

_____

(Signed)

PICTURE OF GRANDMOTHER
AS A YOUNG WOMAN

Write your own caption: _____

_____

_____.

Note to grandparents: You may mount a copy of a photograph on this page and/or you may ask your grandchild to draw a portrait or illustration based on your description.

GRANDFATHER
AS A YOUNG MAN

I began high school in the year _____. I attended _____

_____ school in _____,
city/state/country

_____

My favorite subjects were _____,

and my least favorite subjects were _____.

I celebrated my Confirmation at _____,
city/state/country

_____ in the year _____.

I especially remember my teacher _____,

because _____

_____

_____

The names of my best friends were _____,

_____.

We enjoyed doing many things together including _____

_____

_____.

I'll never forget the time _____

_____

_____

_____.

I'll never forget the time _____

_____

_____

_____.

I was especially proud of _____

_____

_____.

I participated in activities, sports, and clubs such as _____

_____

_____.

The names of our teams/clubs were _____

_____

_____.

My position was _____.

Some of our best programs/activities/games were _____

_____

_____.

The elections/awards I won were for _____

_____

_____.

In those days, my favorite song was _____,

my favorite dance was _____, and my favorite

entertainment (show, program, movie, game, etc.) was _____

_____

_____.

I was a fan of _____

_____.

The most popular fads were _____

_____

_____.

The important world news events of the time were _____

_____

_____

_____.

I remember _____

_____

_____

_____.

I finished high school in _____ and went on to
                                        date
_____. My first "real job" was _____

_____.

My salary was $ _____ per _____. The first election

I voted in was in the year _____, and the candidate I voted

for was _____. _____

was elected. The way I came to choose my occupation of _____

_____ was _____

_____

_____.

I got my training _____

_____.

I belonged to _____ (clubs and organizations).

The Jewish organizations I belonged to were _____

_____

_____.

Some of my activities included _____

_____

_____.

I met your Grandmother in _____. I'll
                                            date
never forget how we met!_____

_____

_____

_____.

The things that attracted me to her were _____

_____

_____.

When we dated _____

_____

_____.

The things I remember most about our courtship were _____

_____

_____

_____.

Other memories of my young adulthood include _____

_____

_____

_____.

_____

(Signed)

PICTURE OF GRANDFATHER
AS A YOUNG MAN

Write your own caption: _____

_____

_____.

Note to grandparents: You may mount a copy of a photograph on this page and/or you may ask your grandchild to draw a portrait or illustration based on your description.

Grant perfect joy to these loving companions.
(Marriage Service)

שַׂמֵחַ תְּשַׂמַח רֵעִים הָאֲהוּבִים

OUR WEDDING AND MARRIAGE
GRANDMOTHER AND GRANDFATHER TOGETHER

We became engaged on _____ in _____,
                              date   city/state/country
and celebrated by _____
_____.

The way it happened was: _____
_____
_____.

Our wedding was on _____ (Hebrew date: _____) in
                          date
_____. Preparations for our wedding included _____
       place
_____
_____.

The officiating rabbi was _____ and the following friends and

relatives participated in the ceremony as witnessess/attendants: _____
_____
_____.

Grandmother wore _____
_____.

and Grandfather wore _____

_____ .

At the ceremony I remember that _____

_____

The reception was _____ ,

_____ .

_____ .

After our wedding we went _____

_____

Our first home was _____ ,
                                  city/state/country

and I would describe it as _____ .

_____ .

Our neighbors were _____ .

During the early years of marriage, Grandfather's occupation was ___

_____ and Grandmother's occupation was

_____ . We bought our first car, a

_____ , in _____ and we took it on its first
                                 date

trip to _____ .

The most exciting thing that happened on that trip was _____

_____ .

In those days, our favorite recipes/foods were _____

prepared by _____ .

Your grandfather's hobbies were _____,

and he belonged to _____.
clubs/organizations

Your grandmother's hobbies were _____,

and she belonged to _____.
clubs/organizations

Our family grew to include

_____, born _____ in _____,
name of child   date   place

who was named after _____. He/she resembled _____.

When he/she was a child _____

_____

_____.

_____, born _____ in _____,
name of child   date   place

who was named after _____. He/she resembled _____.

When he/she was a child _____

_____

_____.

_____, born _____ in _____,
name of child   date   place

who was named after _____. He/she resembled _____.

When he/she was a child _____

_____

_____.

Some families move to new places or homes. We lived in the following

places: _____

_____.

As a family, we enjoyed doing the following things together: _____

_____

_____.

The most memorable trips we took together were to _____

_____

_____,

where we saw _____

_____

_____.

Our closest friends and neighbors were named _____

and with them we enjoyed _____

_____.

Our extended family got together on the following occasions: _____

_____

_____,

at which time we _____

_____.

The synagogue we attended was named _____.

I remember _____

_____

_____.

Note to grandparents: If you do not have enough space on this page, feel free to attach an additional page.

_____

(Signed)

GRANDMOTHER
LOOKING BACK

So far, the most exciting thing that happened to me in my lifetime was

_____

_____

_____

_____

_____.

The best thing that ever happened to me was _____

_____

_____

_____

. . . . But the worst thing I ever experienced was _____

_____

_____

_____.

The way I got through it was _____

_____

_____

_____.

The most difficult thing I ever had to do was _____
_____
_____
_____ .

The thing I am proudest about in my life is _____
_____
_____
_____ .

The most important influence in my life has been _____
_____
_____
_____ .

_____

(Signed)
Grandmother

GRANDFATHER
LOOKING BACK

So far, the most exciting thing that happened to me in my lifetime was

_____

_____

_____

_____.

The best thing that ever happened to me was _____

_____

_____

_____

. . . . But the worst thing I ever experienced was _____

_____

_____

_____.

The way I got through it was _____

_____

_____

_____.

66

The most difficult thing I ever had to do was _____

_____

_____

_____.

The thing I am proudest about in my life is _____

_____

_____

_____.

The most important influence in my life has been _____

_____

_____

_____

_____.

_____

(Signed)
Grandfather

ALL ABOUT YOUR PARENTS

YOUR PARENT/OUR CHILD

(Your Parent as a Baby)

Your _____ was our _____ child. His/her brothers
_{mother/father}   _{1st, 2nd, etc.}

and sisters (in order of birth) were _____

_____.

He/she was born on _____ at ____ o'clock in _____.
     _{date}   _{time}   _{place}

Your parent's vital statistics at birth were: length _____, weight

_____, eye color _____, hair color _____.

Every family has favorite stories about the events accompanying the

birth of their children. When your parent was born _____

_____

_____

_____.

When he/she was born he/she looked like _____

_____.

When we held him/her the first time _____

_____.

When Jewish babies are born it is traditional to hold religious

celebrations (Brit Milah, Pidyon HaBen, Shalom Zachar, Naming,

Simchat Bat). When your parent was born, he/she received his/her

Hebrew name (_____) at _____ on _____.
                      _{celebration}   _{date}

That name was chosen because _____

_____. The people who participated in

the ceremony were _____

_____ .

We celebrated by _____

_____ .

As a baby, he/she had the habit of _____

_____ .

As a baby, his/her favorite toy was _____ ,

and his/her most prized possession was _____ .

The first word your parent spoke was _____ .

Most babies have their own words. Your parent said: _____

_____ .

His/her favorite rhyme was _____ ,

his/her favorite song was _____ ,

and his/her favorite story was _____ .

Your parent was a_____ eater. His/her favorite foods
                    good/poor

were _____ ,

and least favorite foods were _____ .

Some other interesting things you might like to know about your par-

ent as a baby are _____

_____

_____

Your Parent as a Child

As a child, your parent was _____.
                              very active/moderately active/placid
Your parent's nickname was _____ because _____

_____.

His/her favorite activities were _____

_____,

and he/she especially liked these games and toys: _____

_____.

He/she always enjoyed our family outings to _____

_____,

when we would _____

_____.

Your parent's closest playmates were _____

_____. They enjoyed many activities together, including

_____

_____.

I'll never forget when _____

_____

_____.

Your mother/father started school at the age of _____. On the

first day of school I felt _____

_____

and he/she felt _____

_____.

As parents, we were proudest when _____

_____.

The most mischievous thing your parent ever did was _____

_____.

We reacted by _____

_____.

Your parent used to wear _____

_____.

I thought he/she looked _____.

Your parent had to help out with chores like _____

_____.

The way he/she felt about it was _____.

Some other things you might like to know about your mother/

father as a child were _____

_____

_____

_____.

YOUR PARENT'S JEWISH EDUCATION

Your mother/father received his/her Jewish education at _____.

He/she was taught subjects including _____

_____.

He/she liked/loved/disliked religious school because _____

_____

and used to _____

_____.

His/her favorite Jewish holiday was _____ because _____

_____.

For many Jewish people, Bar/Bat Mitzvah is a very important milestone in their lives because it marks the beginning of their Jewish adulthood. Your parent's Bar/Bat Mitzvah was held at_____
                                                              place
on _____. He/she prepared for the occasion by _____
       date
_____.

The rabbi was named _____ and the cantor was _____

_____. That week the Torah portion was _____. Your

mother/father participated by _____

_____.

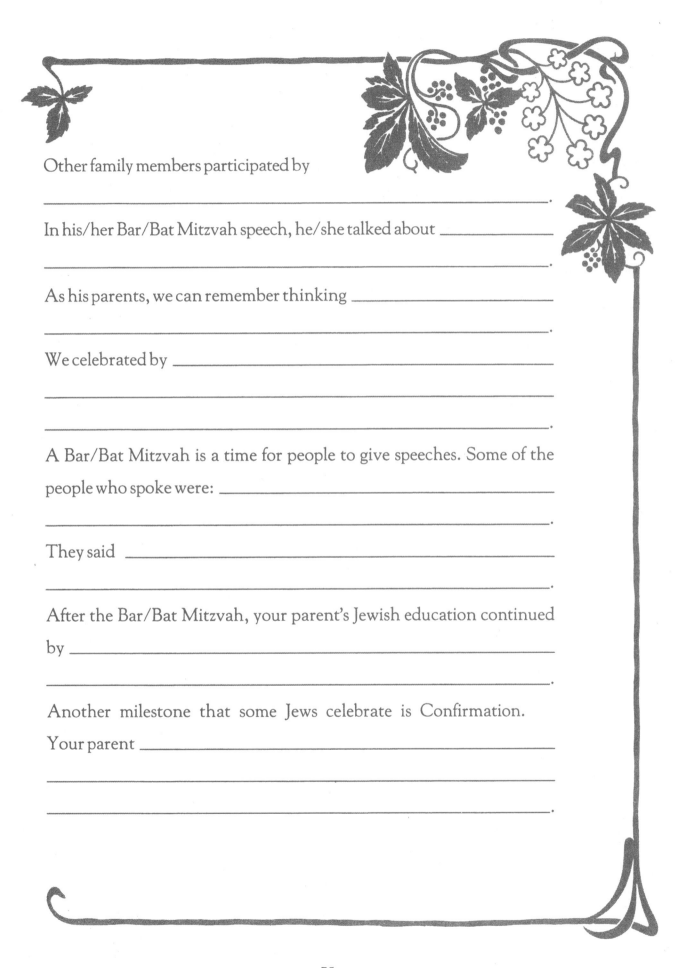

Other family members participated by

_____.

In his/her Bar/Bat Mitzvah speech, he/she talked about _____

_____.

As his parents, we can remember thinking _____

_____.

We celebrated by _____

_____

_____.

A Bar/Bat Mitzvah is a time for people to give speeches. Some of the

people who spoke were: _____

_____.

They said _____

_____.

After the Bar/Bat Mitzvah, your parent's Jewish education continued

by _____

_____.

Another milestone that some Jews celebrate is Confirmation.

Your parent _____

_____

_____.

75

YOUR PARENT AS A TEENAGER

When your parent was a teenager, he/she was especially interested in
_____.

We were especially proud of _____
_____.

Some of the fads we disagreed about were _____
_____.

We used to enjoy discussing _____
_____.

We agreed about _____
_____.

We disagreed about _____
_____.

Your parent moved away from home when _____
_____.

We had to get used to _____
_____.

YOUR PARENT AS A YOUNG ADULT

The first time we met the person your parent planned to marry was

_____

_____.

We thought _____

_____.

All through their courtship _____.

They told us of their wedding plans on _____ by _____.
                                              date

The wedding was on _____ at _____
                        date   place

in _____. The people participating were _____
      city/state

_____

_____

_____

_____.

The things we remember most about the wedding were _____

_____

_____

_____.

After they were married your parents lived in _____.

The first time we visited their new home was _____

_____.

We would get together _____

_____.

Some of our fondest memories are _____

_____

_____

_____.

_____

(Signed)

Wedding Picture
of Your Parents

Write your own caption: _____

_____

_____.

Note to grandparents: You may mount a copy of a photograph on this page and/or you may ask your grandchild to draw a portrait or illustration based on your descriptions.

Parents' Ketubah

_____

And

_____

Were Married

at _____

on the _____ day of _____

in the year 19____ corresponding to the Hebrew date of the_____

day of _____ in the year 57 _____

According to the Laws of the State of
_____ and in accordance with the laws of Moses
and the people Israel.

_____

Rabbi

_____   _____

Bride   Bridegroom

Witnesses: _____

_____

Note to grandparents: If it is not possible to mount a copy of their ketubah, the important information can be filled in on this facsimile.

*Here is a photocopy of your parents' ketubah
(wedding contract).*

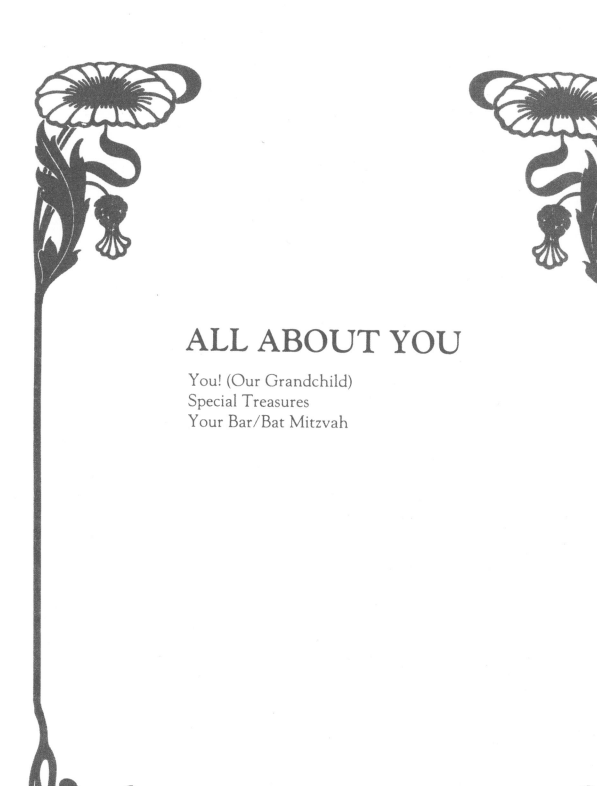

ALL ABOUT YOU

You! (Our Grandchild)
Special Treasures
Your Bar/Bat Mitzvah

Grandchildren are the garlands of their grandparents.
(Proverbs 17:6)

עֲטֶרֶת זְקֵנִים בְּנֵי בָנִים

YOU! (OUR GRANDCHILD)

We learned that you were expected when _____

_____

_____.

Our reaction was _____

_____

_____.

We spent the time awaiting your arrival _____

_____

_____.

We learned of your birth on _____ at _____. We
                             date   time

were _____

_____

_____.

Our first reactions were _____

_____

_____

_____.

The first time we saw you, we thought _____

_____

_____

_____

We said _____

_____

_____.

You were _____

_____

The first time we held you outside the hospital _____

_____.

Compared to your parent, _____

_____.

We celebrated your arrival with the Jewish ceremony (ceremonies) of

_____

_____.

We especially remember _____

_____.

The first time we were alone with you we _____

_____.

We felt _____

_____.

As a baby, you _____

_____.

You did some very cute things. The ones we remember best are _____

_____.

When you grew up to be a toddler _____

_____.

The first Jewish holiday we celebrated with you was _____.

We remember _____

_____.

We were so proud when _____

_____.

When you were very young there were many things we liked to do

together. We used to _____

_____

_____.

The songs we liked to sing together were _____

_____.

You especially liked it when I told you the stories about _____

_____.

The places we especially enjoyed going to together were _____

_____

_____.

Our favorite games to play together were _____

_____

_____.

I remember the time _____

_____

_____.

_____

(Signed)

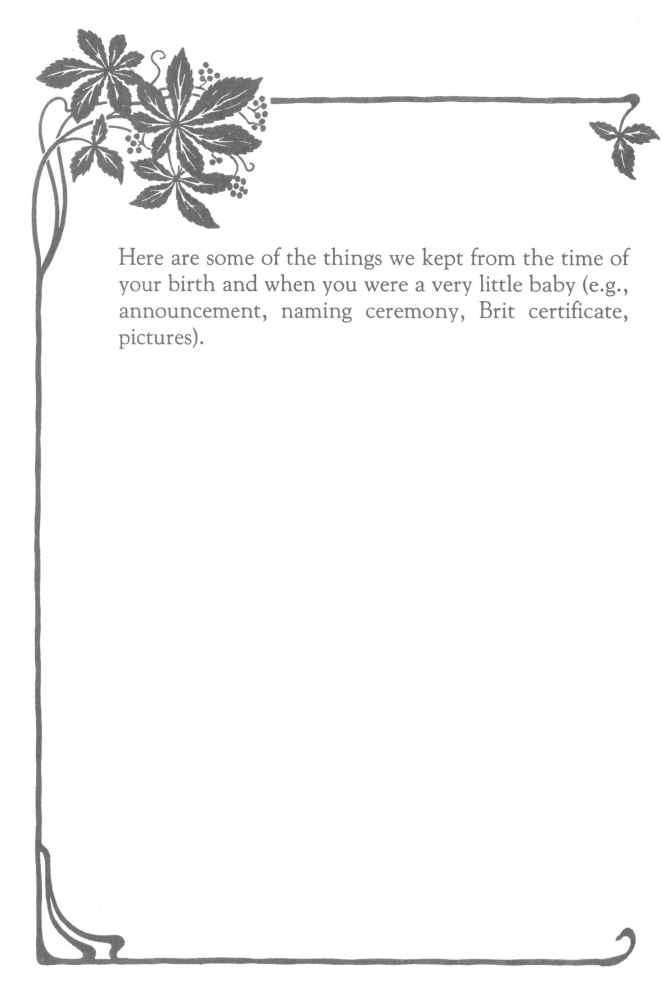

Here are some of the things we kept from the time of your birth and when you were a very little baby (e.g., announcement, naming ceremony, Brit certificate, pictures).

Now that you are older we share interests in _____

_____

_____.

We especially enjoy it when we _____

_____

_____.

We are very proud of your accomplishments in secular school, religious school, and extra curricular activities. Some of the things that gave us the most "naches" (pleasure) include _____

_____

_____

_____

_____

_____

_____

_____

_____

_____

_____.

_____

(Signed)

SOME PICTURES OF YOU WITH US!

Write your own caption:_____

_____

_____

Write your own caption:_____

_____

_____

Write your own caption:_____

_____

_____

Write your own caption:_____

_____

_____

SPECIAL TREASURES

Over the years you have given and sent us many things that we have saved, including gifts, cards, letters, compositions, pictures, report cards, newspaper clippings, and articles.

Item _____

Date received _____

Comment _____

_____

_____

_____

Item _____

Date received _____

Comment _____

_____

_____

_____

Item _____

Date received _____

Comment _____

_____

_____

_____

Item _____

Date received _____

Comment _____

_____

_____

_____

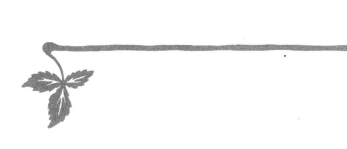

Item _____

Date received _____

Comment _____

_____

_____

_____

_____

_____

_____

Item _____

Date received _____

Comment _____

_____

_____

_____

_____

_____

_____

Item _____

Date received _____

Comment _____

_____

_____

_____

_____

_____

_____

Item _____

Date received _____

Comment _____

_____

_____

_____

_____

_____

_____

At 13, one is ready for Mitzvot.
(Ethics of Our Fathers 5:23)

בֶּן שָׁלוֹשׁ עֶשְׂרֵה לְמִצְוֹת

YOUR BAR/BAT MITZVAH

For a grandparent, the years seem to fly by. Although it seems like such a short time has passed since you were born, you have now become a Bar/Bat Mitzvah. The date on the secular calendar was _____ and the Hebrew date was _____. The weekly portion was _____.   Here is the invitation that we received.

Sitting in the synagogue, we felt _____

_____.

We remembered _____

_____.

We hoped _____

_____.

When you led your parts, we _____

_____.

We were especially proud when _____

_____.

There were many memorable parts of the service. We will always

remember _____

_____

_____.

There are usually many speeches at a Bar/Bat Mitzvah. Some of the

people who spoke at your Bar Mitzvah were _____

_____.

A Bar/Bat Mitzvah is an occasion that brings family and friends to-

gether. We were especially glad to see _____

_____.

It is customary to have a "seudat mitzvah" (festive meal) after a Bar/Bat

Mitzvah. Your celebration was held at _____.
                                            (place)
The festivities included _____

_____

_____.

_____

(Signed)

PICTURES FROM
YOUR BAR/BAT MITZVAH

Write your own caption:_____

_____

_____

Write your own caption:_____

_____

_____

Write your own caption:_____

_____

_____

Write your own caption:_____

_____

_____

HOW WE CELEBRATE

Jewish Holidays
American Holidays

And you shall rejoice before the Lord your God, you, and your son, and your daughter. (Deuteronomy 16:11)

וְשָׂמַחְתָּ לִפְנֵי ה׳ אֱלוֹהֶיךָ אַתָּה וּבִנְךָ וּבִתֶּךָ

Jewish Holidays

Holidays have been very special times for our family throughout the generations. Many traditions remain the same, but with each branch of the family tree new holiday customs and memories are added.

The following pages tell the story of our chain of family celebrations: our holiday preparations, our favorite foods, our special family customs, our most popular holiday songs, the ritual items we use and how we got them, family gatherings that we especially remember, memorable events that occurred on or close to the holidays, pictures and photographs from our family gatherings.

Note to the grandparents: The questions on the following pages are intended to guide your reminiscences about the holidays. Please feel free to use them only as an outline, describing your personal recollections and reactions. There is also a place to record your grandchild's holiday reflections.

Blow the shofar at the new moon, at the appointed season, for our festival day. (Psalm 81:4)

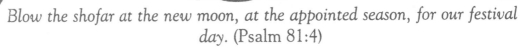

ROSH HASHANAH/YOM KIPPUR

Some special memories of the holidays when I was growing up

Holiday Preparations

(e.g., Did you get new clothes? Did you send special greetings? What were they like?)

Favorite Foods

(e.g., Did your family eat certain foods each Rosh HaShanah or Yom Kippur eve or to break the fast? You may wish to include the recipes in the Recipe section of this book.)

Special Family Customs

(e.g., Did you invite special guests? Did you observe the Tashlich ceremony of symbolically tossing sins into a river or stream?)

Most Popular Melodies

(e.g., Which are your favorite melodies or prayers?)

_____

_____

_____

_____

_____

_____

_____

_____

_____

_____

_____

_____

_____

_____

_____

_____

_____

_____

Some special memories of the holidays when your parent was growing up	Some special memories of the holidays now that you have arrived	A special place for you (my grandchild) to add your own memories and/or pictures of the holidays

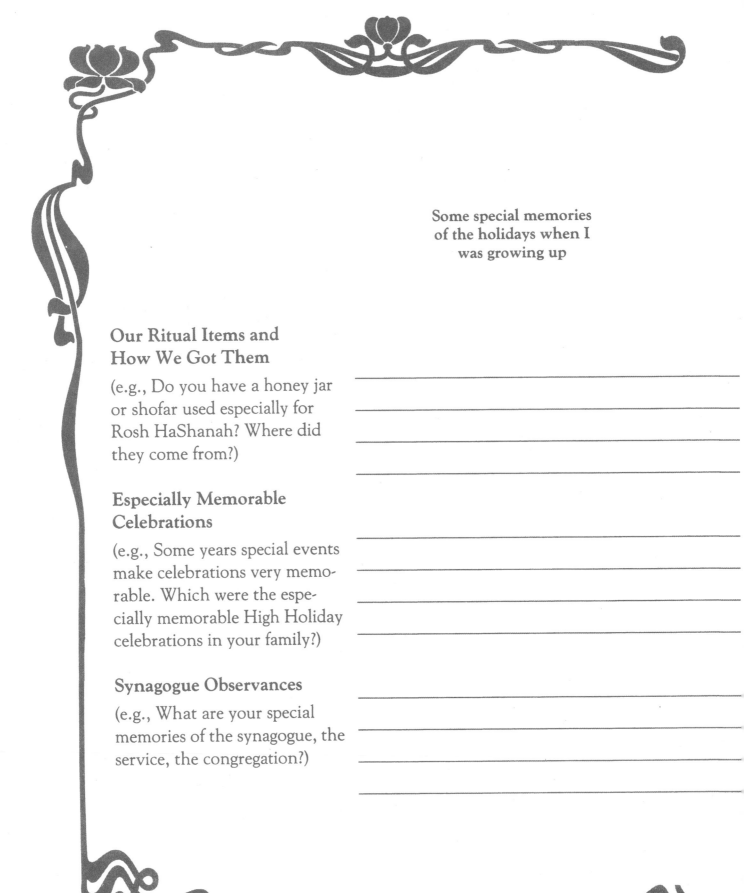

**Some special memories
of the holidays when I
was growing up**

Our Ritual Items and How We Got Them

(e.g., Do you have a honey jar or shofar used especially for Rosh HaShanah? Where did they come from?)

Especially Memorable Celebrations

(e.g., Some years special events make celebrations very memorable. Which were the especially memorable High Holiday celebrations in your family?)

Synagogue Observances

(e.g., What are your special memories of the synagogue, the service, the congregation?)

Some special memories of the holidays when your parent was growing up	Some special memories of the holidays now that you have arrived	A special place for you (my grandchild) to add your own memories and/or pictures of the holidays

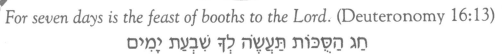

For seven days is the feast of booths to the Lord. (Deuteronomy 16:13)

חַג הַסֻּכּוֹת תַּעֲשֶׂה לְךָ שִׁבְעַת יָמִים

I will exalt and rejoice with the Torah. It is our strength and light.

SUKKOT/SIMCHAT TORAH

**Some special memories
of the holidays when I
was growing up**

Holiday Preparations

(e.g., Did you build a sukkah?
Describe it. Did you buy a lulav
and etrog? Where did you get
them? Did you make flags on
Simchat Torah? Did you put
apples and candles on top?)

_____

_____

_____

_____

Favorite Foods

(e.g., Is it your custom to eat
kreplach/stuffed
cabbage/teiglach/nuts? Did
you ever make etrog jam? You
may wish to include the recipes
in the Recipe section of this
book.)

_____

_____

_____

_____

Most Popular Songs

(e.g., Which are your favorite
Simchat Torah songs for the
hakafot [processionals] with the
Torah?)

_____

_____

_____

_____

_____

Some special memories of the holidays when your parent was growing up	Some special memories of the holidays now that you have arrived	A special place for you (my grandchild) to add your own memories and/or pictures of the holidays

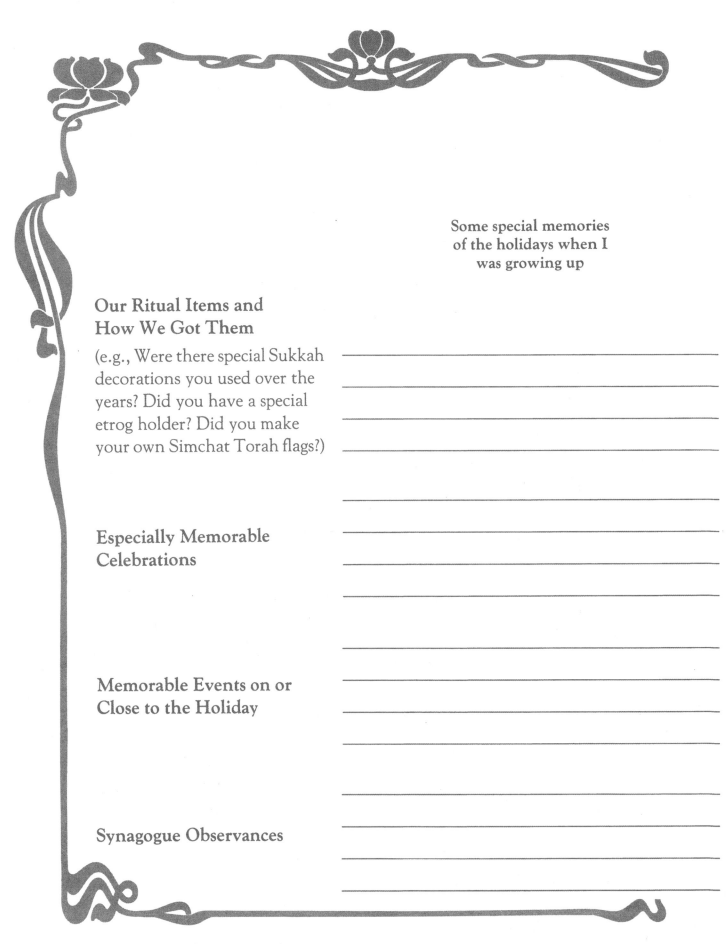

Some special memories
of the holidays when I
was growing up

**Our Ritual Items and
How We Got Them**

(e.g., Were there special Sukkah
decorations you used over the
years? Did you have a special
etrog holder? Did you make
your own Simchat Torah flags?)

**Especially Memorable
Celebrations**

**Memorable Events on or
Close to the Holiday**

Synagogue Observances

Some special memories of the holidays when your parent was growing up	Some special memories of the holidays now that you have arrived	A special place for you (my grandchild) to add your own memories and/or pictures of the holidays

Rock of Ages let our song praise Thy saving power. (Ma'oz Tzur)

מָעוֹז צוּר יְשׁוּעָתִי לְךָ נָאֶה לְשַׁבֵּחַ

Hanukah

**Some special memories
of the holidays when I
was growing up**

Holiday Preparations

(e.g., How did you decorate your home for Hanukah?)

Favorite Foods

(e.g., Did you always have potato latkes? Did you ever eat sufganiot [jelly donuts] like they do in Israel? Did you ever make special Hanukah cookies? Be sure to include your recipes in the Recipe section of this book.)

Special Family Customs

(e.g., What was your family tradition for the ceremony of lighting the candles? What were your family traditions regarding gift giving? Did you give Hanukah gelt? Were there any especially memorable gifts? What kinds of games did you play? Did you play dreidel for nuts, pennies, or something else? Did you tell Hanukah stories or put on plays?)

Some special memories of the holidays when your parent was growing up	Some special memories of the holidays now that you have arrived	A special place for you (my grandchild) to add your own memories and/or pictures of the holidays

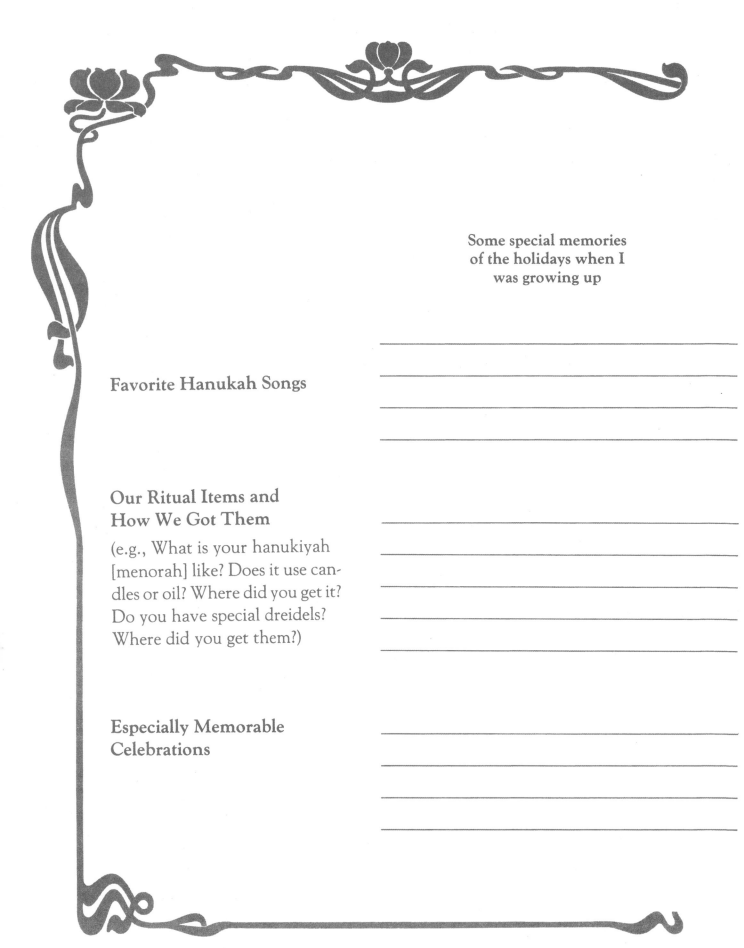

**Some special memories
of the holidays when I
was growing up**

Favorite Hanukah Songs

Our Ritual Items and
How We Got Them

(e.g., What is your hanukiyah
[menorah] like? Does it use candles or oil? Where did you get it?
Do you have special dreidels?
Where did you get them?)

Especially Memorable
Celebrations

Some special memories of the holidays when your parent was growing up	Some special memories of the holidays now that you have arrived	A special place for you (my grandchild) to add your own memories and/or pictures of the holidays

With the beginning of Adar, rejoicing is increased. (Taanit 29a)

מִשֶׁנִּכְנַס אֲדָר מַרְבִּין בְּשִׂמְחָה

PURIM

**Some special memories
of the holidays when I
was growing up**

Holiday Preparations

(e.g., What were some of your
best costumes? Did you prepare
shalach manot — "goody"
baskets — for your friends and
family? What did you include in
them? How were they deliv-
ered? Did you send matanot
l'evyonim [gifts to the needy]?)

_____

_____

_____

_____

_____

_____

Favorite Foods

(e.g., Which kinds of
hamantashen were your favorites? Be sure to include the recipes in the Recipe section of this
book. Did you have a Purim
seudah [meal]? What was
served?)

_____

_____

_____

_____

_____

Favorite Purim Songs

_____

_____

_____

_____

Some special memories of the holidays when your parent was growing up	Some special memories of the holidays now that you have arrived	A special place for you (my grandchild) to add your own memories and/or pictures of the holidays

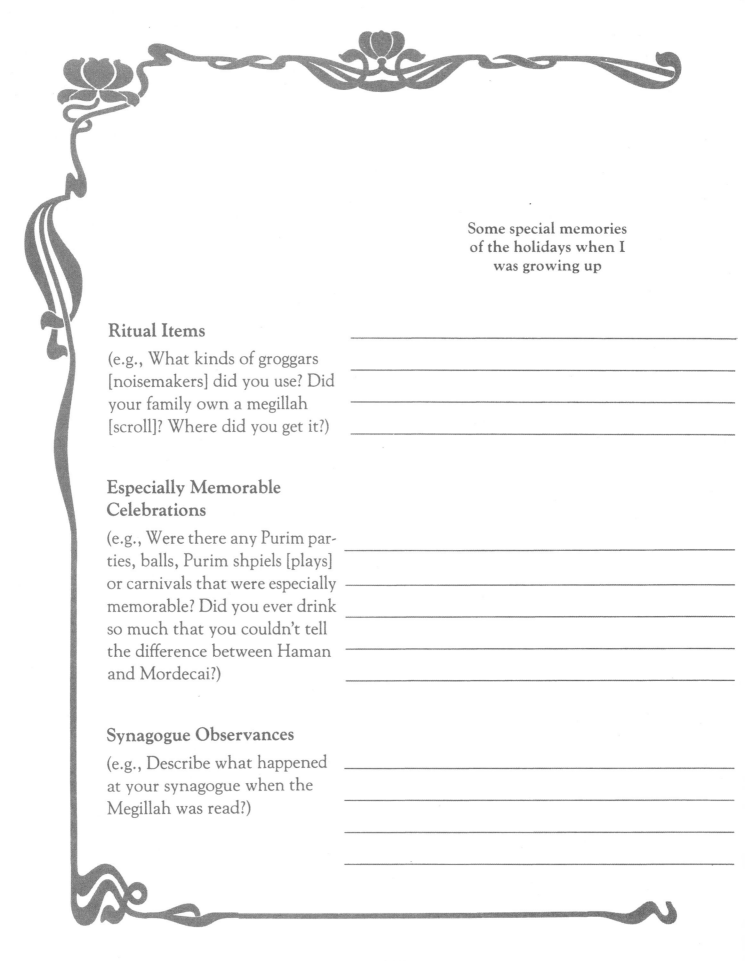

Some special memories
of the holidays when I
was growing up

Ritual Items

(e.g., What kinds of groggars [noisemakers] did you use? Did your family own a megillah [scroll]? Where did you get it?)

Especially Memorable Celebrations

(e.g., Were there any Purim parties, balls, Purim shpiels [plays] or carnivals that were especially memorable? Did you ever drink so much that you couldn't tell the difference between Haman and Mordecai?)

Synagogue Observances

(e.g., Describe what happened at your synagogue when the Megillah was read?)

Some special memories of the holidays when your parent was growing up	Some special memories of the holidays now that you have arrived	A special place for you (my grandchild) to add your own memories and/or pictures of the holidays

In every generation everyone ought to look upon himself as if he personally had come out of Egypt. (Passover Haggadah)

בְּכָל דּוֹר וָדוֹר חַיָּב אָדָם לִרְאוֹת אֶת עַצְמוֹ כְּאִלּוּ הוּא יָצָא מִמִּצְרַיִם

PASSOVER

Some special memories of the holidays when I was growing up

Holiday Preparations

(e.g., When did housecleaning begin for Passover? What had to be done? Who helped? To whom did you sell your hametz [leavened foods]? Did you participate in the Fast of the Firstborn? Did you give ma'ot hittim [charity]? If so, what was your usual charity?)

Favorite Foods

(e.g., Did you have a traditional seder menu in your family? Who did the cooking? Did you prefer hard or soft matzah balls? What was your favorite Passover delicacy? Did you prefer a special type of matzah?)

Some special memories of the holidays when your parent was growing up	Some special memories of the holidays now that you have arrived	A special place for you (my grandchild) to add your own memories and/or pictures of the holidays

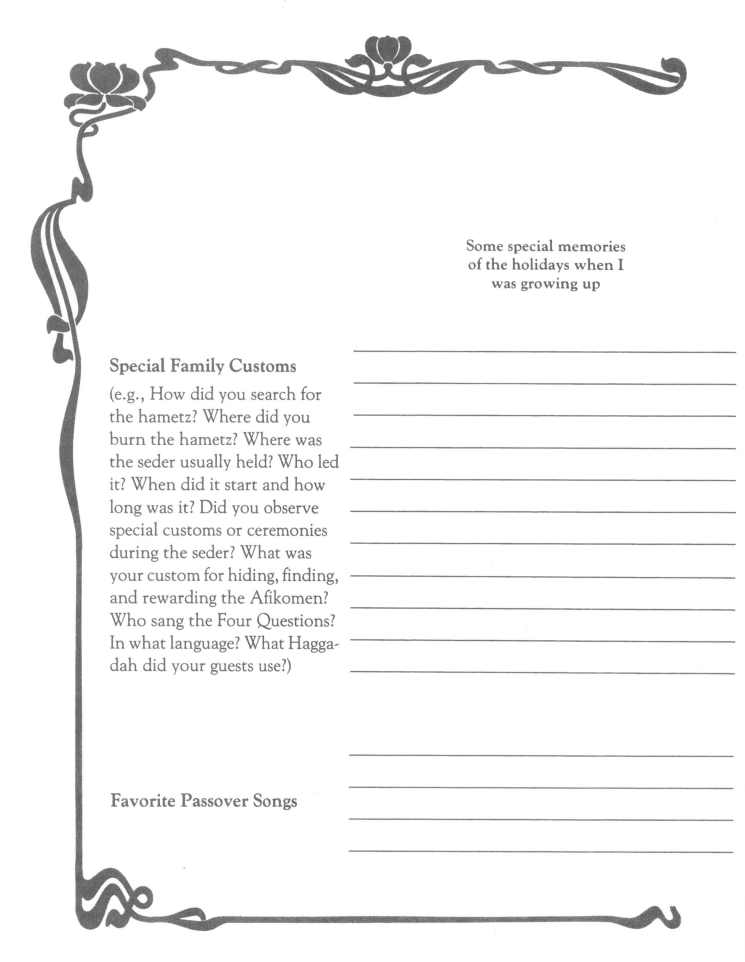

Some special memories
of the holidays when I
was growing up

Special Family Customs

(e.g., How did you search for
the hametz? Where did you
burn the hametz? Where was
the seder usually held? Who led
it? When did it start and how
long was it? Did you observe
special customs or ceremonies
during the seder? What was
your custom for hiding, finding,
and rewarding the Afikomen?
Who sang the Four Questions?
In what language? What Haggadah did your guests use?)

Favorite Passover Songs

Some special memories of the holidays when your parent was growing up	Some special memories of the holidays now that you have arrived	A special place for you (my grandchild) to add your own memories and/or pictures of the holidays

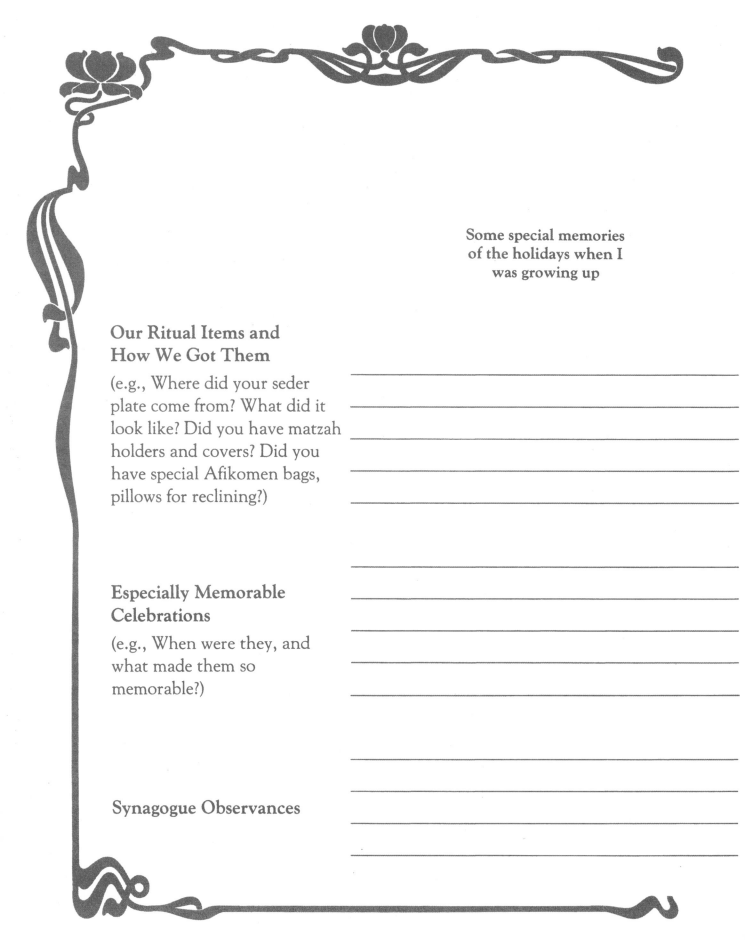

**Some special memories
of the holidays when I
was growing up**

Our Ritual Items and
How We Got Them

(e.g., Where did your seder
plate come from? What did it
look like? Did you have matzah
holders and covers? Did you
have special Afikomen bags,
pillows for reclining?)

Especially Memorable
Celebrations

(e.g., When were they, and
what made them so
memorable?)

Synagogue Observances

Some special memories of the holidays when your parent was growing up	Some special memories of the holidays now that you have arrived	A special place for you (my grandchild) to add your own memories and/or pictures of the holidays

On the day of the first fruits, your Feast of Weeks, when you bring an offering of new grain to the Lord, you shall observe a sacred occasion.
(Numbers 28:26)

וּבְיוֹם הַבִּכּוּרִים בְּהַקְרִיבְכֶם מִנְחָה חֲדָשָׁה לַה׳ בְּשָׁבֻעֹתֵיכֶם מִקְרָא קֹדֶשׁ יִהְיֶה לָכֶם

SHAVUOT

Some special memories
of the holidays when I
was growing up

_____

Favorite Foods

(e.g., Did you eat blintzes?
What other dairy foods were
your family's favorites?)

_____
_____
_____
_____

**Especially Memorable
Celebrations**

(e.g., Did you or any family
members participate in a confirmation ceremony?)

_____
_____
_____
_____

Synagogue Observances

(e.g., Did you ever participate in
a Tikkun Leil Shavuot [all-
night study session]? Describe
it.)

_____
_____
_____
_____

Some special memories of the holidays when your parent was growing up	Some special memories of the holidays now that you have arrived	A special place for you (my grandchild) to add your own memories and/or pictures of the holidays

It is a sign between Me and the children of Israel forever. (Exodus 31:17)

בֵּינִי וּבֵין בְּנֵי יִשְׂרָאֵל אוֹת הִיא לְעוֹלָם

Shabbat

**Some special memories
of the holidays when I
was growing up**

Holiday Preparations

(e.g., How did you prepare
[cleaning, cooking, etc.] for the
Sabbath? Did you bake
hallahs?)

_____

_____

_____

_____

Favorite Foods

(e.g., Were there special menus
for the Sabbath eve? Were there
special menus for Sabbath
lunch or the seudah shlishit
[Saturday afternoon meal]?
What were your favorite recipes? Be sure to include them in
the Recipe section of this book.)

_____

_____

_____

_____

_____

_____

Special Family Customs

(e.g., Describe your family's
Sabbath ritual [blessings, meal,
singing, discussions, stories,
games, services]. How did you
celebrate the Sabbath day? Did
you have a special Havdalah
ceremony to end the Sabbath?)

_____

_____

_____

_____

_____

_____

Some special memories of the holidays when your parent was growing up	Some special memories of the holidays now that you have arrived	A special place for you (my grandchild) to add your own memories and/or pictures of the holidays.

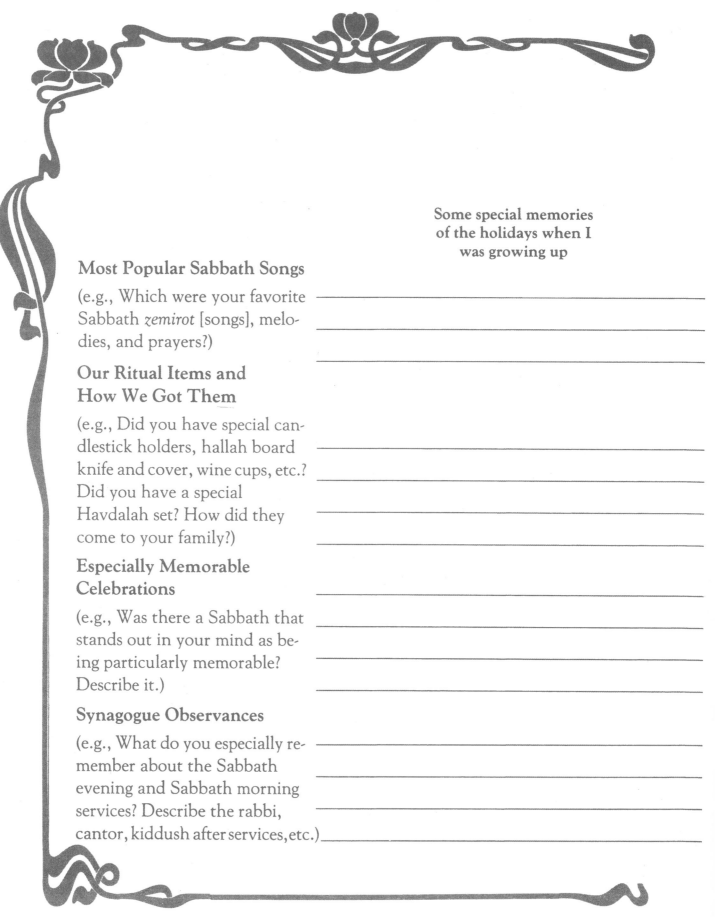

**Some special memories
of the holidays when I
was growing up**

Most Popular Sabbath Songs

(e.g., Which were your favorite Sabbath *zemirot* [songs], melodies, and prayers?)

Our Ritual Items and How We Got Them

(e.g., Did you have special candlestick holders, hallah board knife and cover, wine cups, etc.? Did you have a special Havdalah set? How did they come to your family?)

Especially Memorable Celebrations

(e.g., Was there a Sabbath that stands out in your mind as being particularly memorable? Describe it.)

Synagogue Observances

(e.g., What do you especially remember about the Sabbath evening and Sabbath morning services? Describe the rabbi, cantor, kiddush after services, etc.)

128

Some special memories of the holidays when your parent was growing up	Some special memories of the holidays now that you have arrived	A special place for you (my grandchild) to add your own memories and/or pictures of the holidays

Here are some other Jewish holidays you may celebrate. If so, describe your celebrations. Here are some examples to help you.

OTHER JEWISH HOLIDAYS

**Some special memories
of the holidays when I
was growing up**

Tu Bishevat

(e.g., Did you plant trees? Did you have a Tu Bishevat seder? Did you eat bokser [St. John's bread, carob], almonds, and dried fruit?)

Lag B'Omer

(e.g., Did you go on picnics and have bonfires?)

Israel Independence Day

(e.g., Did you attend Israel Independence Day celebrations? Describe them.)

Other

Some special memories of the holidays when your parent was growing up	Some special memories of the holidays now that you have arrived	A special place for you (my grandchild) to add your own memories and/or pictures of the holidays

AMERICAN HOLIDAYS

**Some special memories
of the holidays when I
was growing up**

THANKSGIVING

Favorite Foods

_____

_____

_____

_____

Special Family Customs

(e.g., With whom did you celebrate? Did you offer a special
Thanksgiving blessing at the
meal? Did you donate food or
money to the needy at this
time?)

_____

_____

_____

_____

Community Celebrations

(e.g., Was there a community
Thanksgiving service that you
attended? Describe it.)

_____

_____

_____

_____

Some special memories of the holidays when your parent was growing up	Some special memories of the holidays now that you have arrived	A special place for you (my grandchild) to add your own memories and/or pictures of the holidays

Some special memories
of the holidays when I
was growing up

FOURTH OF JULY
Favorite Foods

(e.g., Did you have a special
barbeque? Describe it.)

_____
_____
_____
_____

Special Family Customs

(e.g., Did you go to see fire-
works displays, parades, or outdoor concerts? Did you ever go
on an outdoor picnic? Describe
it.)

_____
_____
_____
_____

Favorite Patriotic Songs

_____
_____
_____
_____
_____

Other

_____
_____

Some special memories of the holidays when your parent was growing up	Some special memories of the holidays now that you have arrived	A special place for you (my grandchild) to add your own memories and/or pictures of the holidays

RECORDS AND TRADITIONS: A FAMILY DIRECTORY

Our Jewish Family Heirlooms
Our Family Holiday Recipes
Other Favorite Family Recipes
Birthdays in Our Family
Wedding Anniversaries in Our Family
Family Address and Telephone Directory
Family Yahrzeit Record: Anniversaries of Death
Our Relatives Who Perished During the Holocaust

From generation to generation. (Amida prayer)

לְדוֹר וָדוֹר

OUR JEWISH FAMILY HEIRLOOMS

Some heirlooms are Jewish ceremonial objects that are used and/or displayed for holidays and other ritual events, like kiddush cups, menorahs, seder plates, havdalah sets, candlesticks, shofars, etc. In some families, these are passed down from generation to generation and have beautiful histories associated with them. These are our family heirlooms and how we got them:

Description of the item _____

How we acquired it _____

_____

_____

Description of the item _____

How we acquired it _____

_____

_____

Description of the item _____

How we acquired it _____

_____

_____

Description of the item _____

How we acquired it _____

_____

_____

Description of the item _____

How we acquired it _____

_____

_____

Description of the item _____

How we acquired it _____

_____

_____

Description of the item _____

How we acquired it _____

_____

_____

And you shall eat and be satisfied.
(Deuteronomy 11:15)

וְאָכַלְתָּ וְשָׂבָעְתָּ

Our Family
Holiday Recipes

Holiday _____   Recipe for _____

Ingredients and Directions

_____

_____

_____

_____

_____

_____

_____

_____

_____

Holiday _____   Recipe for _____

Ingredients and Directions

_____

_____

_____

_____

_____

_____

_____

_____

Holiday _____   Recipe for _____

Ingredients and Directions

_____

_____

_____

_____

_____

_____

_____

_____

_____

_____

Holiday _____   Recipe for _____

Ingredients and Directions

_____

_____

_____

_____

_____

_____

_____

_____

OTHER FAVORITE FAMILY RECIPES

Recipe for _____

Ingredients and Directions

_____

_____

_____

_____

_____

_____

_____

_____

Recipe for _____

Ingredients and Directions

_____

_____

_____

_____

_____

_____

_____

_____

_____

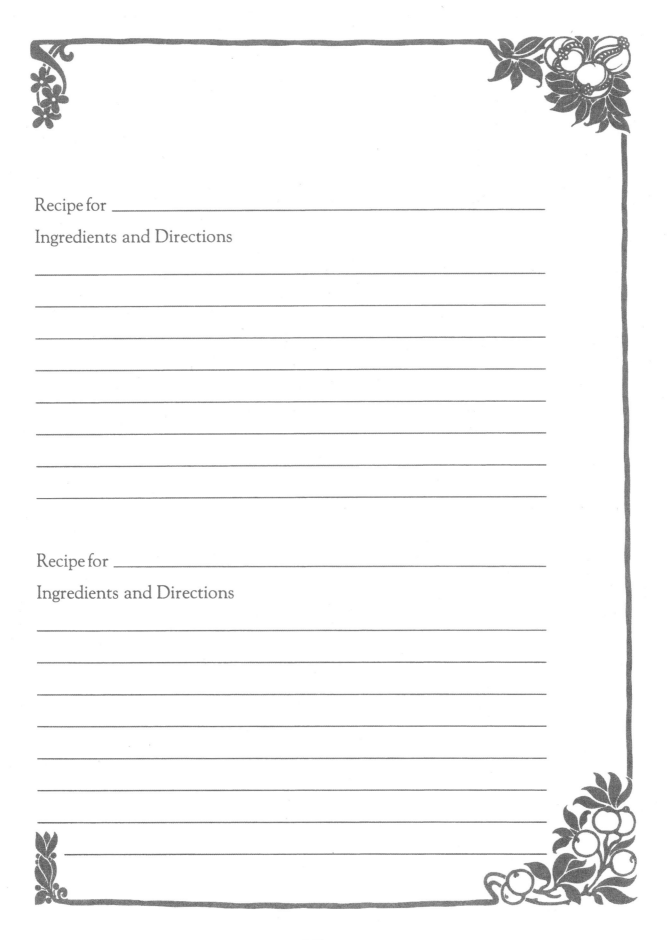

Recipe for _____

Ingredients and Directions

_____
_____
_____
_____
_____
_____
_____
_____

Recipe for _____

Ingredients and Directions

_____
_____
_____
_____
_____
_____
_____
_____
_____

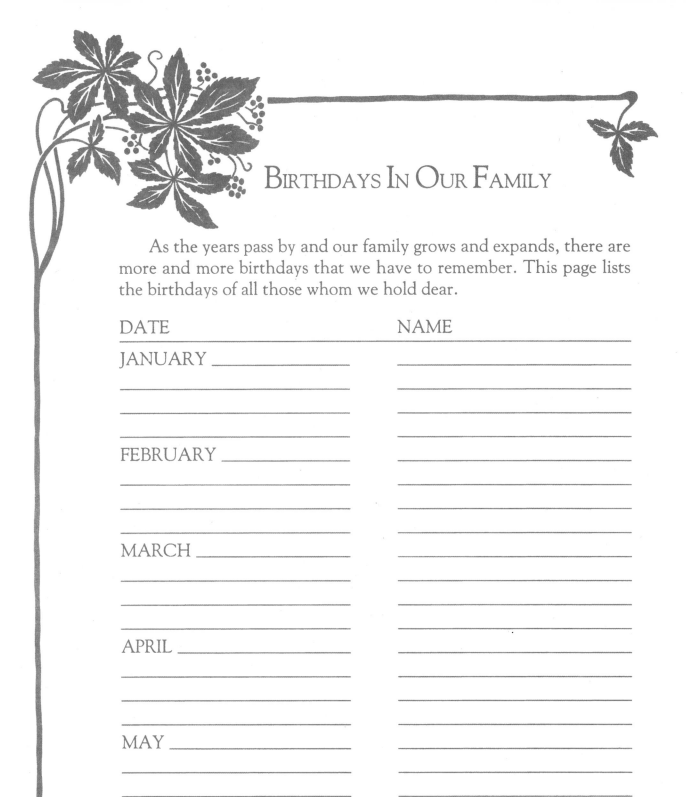

BIRTHDAYS IN OUR FAMILY

As the years pass by and our family grows and expands, there are more and more birthdays that we have to remember. This page lists the birthdays of all those whom we hold dear.

DATE _____   NAME _____

JANUARY _____   _____

_____   _____

_____   _____

FEBRUARY _____   _____

_____   _____

_____   _____

MARCH _____   _____

_____   _____

_____   _____

APRIL _____   _____

_____   _____

_____   _____

MAY _____   _____

_____   _____

_____   _____

JUNE _____   _____

_____   _____

_____   _____

DATE   NAME

JULY _____   _____
_____   _____
_____   _____

AUGUST _____   _____
_____   _____
_____   _____

SEPTEMBER _____   _____
_____   _____
_____   _____

OCTOBER _____   _____
_____   _____
_____   _____

NOVEMBER _____   _____
_____   _____
_____   _____

DECEMBER _____   _____
_____   _____
_____   _____

My soul takes pleasure in three things, for they are beautiful to the Lord and to all men: harmony among brothers, friendship among neighbors, and a husband and wife suited to each other. (Ben Sira 25:1)

WEDDING ANIVERSARIES IN OUR FAMILY

We have fond memories of celebrating our own wedding anniversary, which is on _____. There are others whose anniversaries we have remembered over these past years as well. These are the anniversary dates of the people who have been so much a part of our lives.

DATE	NAME
JANUARY _____	_____
_____	_____
_____	_____
_____	_____
FEBRUARY _____	_____
_____	_____
_____	_____
_____	_____
MARCH _____	_____
_____	_____
_____	_____
APRIL _____	_____
_____	_____
_____	_____
_____	_____
MAY _____	_____
_____	_____
_____	_____
_____	_____

DATE _____ NAME _____

JUNE _____ _____

_____ _____

_____ _____

_____ _____

JULY _____ _____

_____ _____

_____ _____

AUGUST _____ _____

_____ _____

_____ _____

SEPTEMBER _____ _____

_____ _____

_____ _____

OCTOBER _____ _____

_____ _____

_____ _____

NOVEMBER _____ _____

_____ _____

_____ _____

DECEMBER _____ _____

_____ _____

_____ _____

_____ _____

FAMILY ADDRESS AND TELEPHONE DIRECTORY

These names, addresses, and telephone numbers will help you keep in touch with our family members:

Name _____

Address _____

_____

Telephone ( ) _____

Name _____

Address _____

_____

Telephone ( ) _____

Name _____

Address _____

_____

Telephone ( ) _____

Name _____

Address _____

_____

Telephone ( ) _____

Name _____

Address _____

_____

Telephone ( ) _____

Name _____

Address _____

_____

Telephone ( ) _____

Name _____   Name _____

Address _____   Address _____

_____   _____

Telephone ( ) _____   Telephone ( ) _____

Name _____   Name _____

Address _____   Address _____

_____   _____

Telephone ( ) _____   Telephone ( ) _____

Name _____   Name _____

Address _____   Address _____

_____   _____

Telephone ( ) _____   Telephone ( ) _____

Grant perfect peace in your Sheltering Presence to the souls of our dear ones. (Yizkor Memorial Service)

FAMILY YAHRZEIT RECORD
ANNIVERSARIES OF DEATH

We recall with affection the members of our family who are no longer with us.

Name _____   Name _____

Relationship _____   Relationship _____

Hebrew Date of Death _____   Hebrew Date of Death _____

Name _____   Name _____

Relationship _____   Relationship _____

Hebrew Date of Death _____   Hebrew Date of Death _____

Name _____

Relationship _____

Hebrew Date of Death _____

Name _____

Relationship _____

Hebrew Date of Death _____

Name _____

Relationship _____

Hebrew Date of Death _____

Name _____

Relationship _____

Hebrew Date of Death _____

Name _____

Relationship _____

Hebrew Date of Death _____

Name _____

Relationship _____

Hebrew Date of Death _____

Name _____

Relationship _____

Hebrew Date of Death _____

Name _____

Relationship _____

Hebrew Date of Death _____

May He be mindful of the souls who sacrificed their lives for the sanctification of the Holy Name and the honor of Israel. (Yizkor Memorial Service)

OUR RELATIVES WHO PERISHED DURING THE HOLOCAUST

Six million Jews were killed during the Holocaust. Very few Jewish families were spared the loss of family members.

In Grandmother's family, these are the names of family members who perished during the Holocaust:

_____

_____

_____

_____

_____

_____

_____

_____

In Grandfather's family these are the names of family members who perished during the Holocaust:

_____

_____

_____

_____

_____

_____

_____

_____

May their souls be bound up in the bond of life. (Yizkor Memorial Service)

FINAL THOUGHTS

REFLECTIONS

The world has changed greatly during our lifetimes. There has been phenomenal progress in transportation, communication, and technology. We have witnessed new developments in entertainment and leisure activities. Family structures and the roles of men and women are different than when we were your age. As Jews, our status has changed remarkably, and while we have suffered the horrors of the Holocaust, we have been privileged to witness the rebirth of the State of Israel. Some of the changes that have affected us the most are:

_____

_____

_____

_____

_____

_____

_____

_____

_____

_____

_____

(Signed)

DID WE
FORGET ANYTHING?

*Are there any questions that you (our grandchild)
would like to ask us (your grandparents)?*

_____

_____

_____

_____

_____

_____

_____

_____

_____

_____

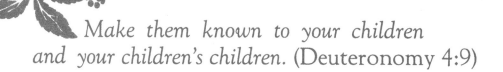

Make them known to your children and your children's children. (Deuteronomy 4:9)

ETHICAL WILL

A most beautiful Jewish custom that is not well known in our time is the writing of an ethical will. Parents and grandparents would write letters to their children and grandchildren expressing their hopes for the future and the values they bequeathed to their descendants. Here is a modern example of an ethical will:

SAM LEVENSON

Sam Levenson was raised and educated in New York. He taught in New York City high schools for fifteen years before making a successful career as a humorist. He became a beloved, nationally known personality through his books and appearances on radio and television; he had his own program, the "Sam Levenson Show," on Columbia Broadcasting System television. The major focus of his humor was the family—raising children and growing up in an urban environment. Some of his writings appear in textbooks on urban sociology. It has been said of his humor that it was of a special kind: it sought laughter at nobody's expense. This is his "Ethical Will and Testament to His Grandchildren, and to Children Everywhere."

I leave you my unpaid debts. They are my greatest assets. Everything I own—I owe:

1. To America I owe a debt for the opportunity it gave me to be free and to be me.

2. To my parents I owe America. They gave it to me and I leave it to you. Take good care of it.

3. To the biblical tradition I owe the belief that man does not live by bread alone, nor does he live alone at all. This is also the democratic tradition. Preserve it.

4. To the six million of my people and to the thirty million other humans who died because of man's inhumanity to man, I owe a vow that it must never happen again.

5. I leave you not everything I never had, but everything I had in my lifetime: a good family, respect for learning, compassion for my fellowman, and some four-letter words for all occasions: words like "help," "give," "care," "feel," and "love."

Love, my dear grandchildren, is easier to recommend than to define. I can tell you only that like those who came before you, you will surely know when love ain't; you will also know when mercy ain't and brotherhood ain't.

The millennium will come when all the "ain'ts" shall have become "ises" and all the "ises" shall be for all, even for those you don't like.

Finally, I leave you the years I should like to have lived so that I might possibly see whether *your* generation will bring more love and peace to the world than ours did. I not only hope you will. I pray that you will.

Grandpa Sam Levenson

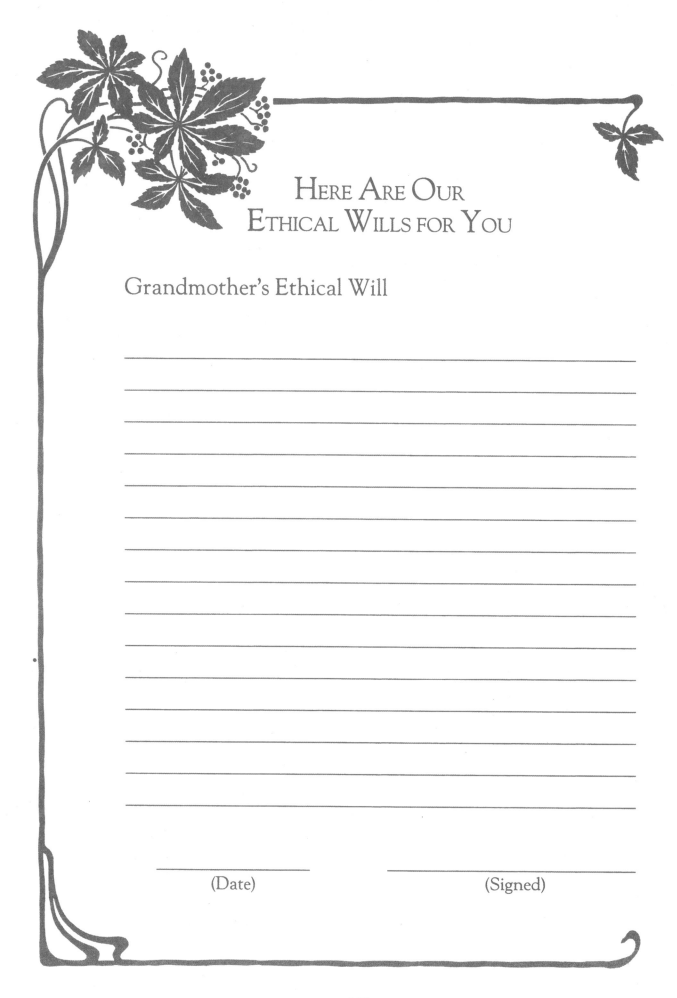

HERE ARE OUR
ETHICAL WILLS FOR YOU

Grandmother's Ethical Will

_____

_____

_____

_____

_____

_____

_____

_____

_____

_____

_____

_____

_____

_____

_____

_____

_____

_____   _____
(Date)   (Signed)

Grandfather's Ethical Will

_____

_____

_____

_____

_____

_____

_____

_____

_____

_____

_____

_____

_____

_____

_____

_____

_____

_____

_____   _____
(Date)   (Signed)

Set me as a seal upon your heart. (Song of Songs 8:6–7)

שִׂימֵנִי כַחוֹתָם עַל לִבֶּךָ

SIGNATURE PAGE

Here are our signatures as we grow together:

_____	_____	_____
Grandchild's 1st Signature	Date	Grandparents' Signatures

Grandchild's Thumbprints	Date	Grandparents' Thumbprints

_____	_____	_____
Grandchild's Signature	Date	Grandparents' Signatures

Helpful hint: Use an ink pad with washable ink to make the thumbprints. You may want to add a signature and thumbprint each year on another page.

A Reflection
From the Talmud

A rabbi was passing through a field when he noticed an elderly man who was planting an acorn.

"Why are you planting that acorn?" he asked. "You surely do not expect to live long enough to see it grow into an oak tree."

The man replied, "My grandparents planted seeds so that I might enjoy the shade and the fruit trees. Now I do likewise for my grandchildren and all those who come after me." (Taanit 23a)